CLOSE COVER BEFORE STRIKING

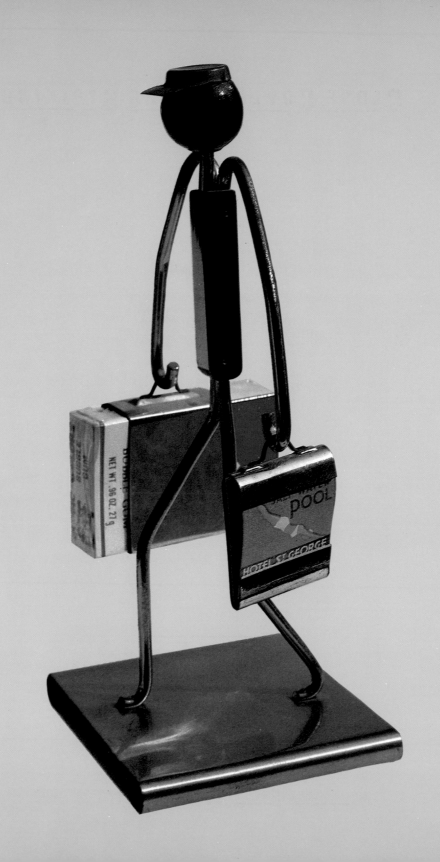

CLOSE COVER BEFORE STRIKING

BY

H. THOMAS STEELE

JIM HEIMANN

ROD DYER

ABBEVILLE PRESS · PUBLISHERS · NEW YORK

DEDICATE**D**

to all non-smokers and to the
safe use of matches

Editor: Walton Rawls
Design: Rod Dyer/Harriet Baba, Dyer/Kahn, Inc.
Principal Photography: H. Thomas Steele
Art Direction: H. Thomas Steele, Jim Heimann

Steele, H. Thomas, 1953-
    Close cover before striking.
     I. Matchcovers—United States—
     Collectors and Collecting.
     2. Matchcovers—United States—
     Themes, Motives.
     I. Heimann, Jim, 1948-
     II. Dyer, Rod, 1935-
     III. Title.
NC1890.U6S74   1987   741.6′9′0973075
86-28787
ISBN 0-89659-695-8

TABLE OF CONTENTS

6	INTRODUCTION
12	ADVERTISING
20	WESTERN
26	GIRLIES
32	TRAVEL
38	HOTELS
44	GENERIC
52	EATERIES
62	NOVELTY
70	PATRIOTISM
76	MOVIELAND
82	ANIMALS
86	EXPOSITIONS
90	SPORTS

Fire, along with air, water, and earth, was long regarded as one of our planet's four basic elements. Essential to life here, it probably first manifested itself to man in a fearsome accident of nature—a forest fire, ignited by lightning, that roared through a rudimentary settlement and then died out. Small animals roasted in the conflagration attracted man's interest and appetite—so the next accidental fire was kept from going out entirely, husbanded on a primitive hearth. Eventually the curious lure of fire taught man to bring it forth when desired, by rubbing dry sticks of wood together continuously until friction raised the temperature of adjacent tinder to the combustion point. Then man learned not only to provide himself with cooked food but warmth when winter winds blew through his cave. From these humble beginnings, man's quest has further transformed the power of fire into such useful devices as the match and the inter-

nal combustion engine—but also into such destructive instruments of warfare as the flamethrower and the nuclear bomb.

Another early fire-making device, flint and steel (which survives today in portable cigarette lighters), sparked us through most of the historical era, including the Industrial Revolution and the Civil War. But it was the discovery of the element phosphorus

in 1669 by the brilliant German alchemist Hannig Brandt that brought forth the match. An element that oxidizes or burns when exposed to air, phosphorus generates enough heat to ignite paper or wood shavings, and in the following two centuries many different attempts were made to use phosphorus in a practical fire-making device. An Englishman named John Walker earned the distinction of inventing the

first friction match in 1827.

Using splinters of wood tipped with sulphur and phosphorus, he ignited an industry. The paper match was the bright idea of a Philadelphia patent attorney named Joshua Pusey. He reasoned that wooden matches were troublesome to carry and that paper burned as well as wood and did not take up as much space. Pusey brewed the chemicals used in making match heads on his office stove, and he dipped thin strips of cardboard into the solution, stapling them to a leftover piece of cardboard. This crude ancestor of the modern matchbook—convenient, affordable, and relatively safe—was patented on September 26, 1892. The Diamond Match Company heard of the invention and offered to buy the patent rights from Pusey for $4,000. Not only did Pusey accept their offer, but he also joined Diamond as their patent attorney, to protect their new patent for the rest of his life.

In 1894 the flames of early

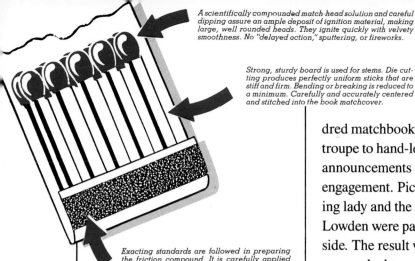

advertising were fanned by a creative match-company salesman named Henry C. Traute. He had heard about the success of a clever idea used by the Mendelssohn Opera Company. With no money left to advertise their upcoming performance in New York City, their manager bought several hundred matchbooks and set the troupe to hand-lettering them with announcements of the pending engagement. Pictures of the leading lady and the comedian Thomas Lowden were pasted on the outside. The result was that the hall was packed to capacity—which was all Traute needed to hear for spawning even greater schemes. On speculation he had a lithographer reprint a magazine advertisement for Pabst beer in matchbook size. He took the ad on the next train to Milwaukee, where he secured an order from Pabst Brewery for 10 million matchbooks with printed covers.

Traute next tried a tobacco firm, but both he and his matchbooks were unceremoniously thrown out the door. He turned to that company's rivals, the producers of Bull Durham, and received an order for 30 million matchbooks! The home office panicked—to fill orders like these, new machinery had to be hastily designed and assembled to supplant the hand-labor force. When Traute returned with orders in the billions, the new equipment was whipping out matchcovers at the rate of 10,000 an hour. One company quickly followed another into this new advertising medium. Billions of matchbooks with beautiful covers hit the market, but the skeptical public refused to buy

OUR MODERN ART STUDIO

them—they were dangerous. Traute had the striking surface moved from inside the matchcover to the outside, a much safer distance from the combustible match heads. Matchbooks were then imprinted with the now familiar "Close Cover Before Striking." Many decades later, in 1962, Federal safety laws required that the striker be moved to the backside of the matchcover, to prevent the user from accidentally creating an incendiary device in his own hands. This transfer of the striker from the front to the back (and the elimination of the memorable slogan) marked the end of an era for collectible matchcovers.

Still the public refused to buy matchbooks even at two packages for a penny. It made Traute wonder if people would use them if they were free. He convinced a New York tobacconist at a corner intersection to give this outlandish idea a try, with the promise of increasing tobacco sales. It worked. Sales of tobacco doubled, and the giveaway practice spread to the West Coast within a short time. Not only did sales increase for the product the matches were given away with, but the product advertised on the matchcover was reintroduced to the minds of consumers every time one of the twenty matches was used. Rarely, it was found, did a matchbook get thrown away before all of the matches were struck. This inexpensive form of advertising was distributed free not only with packs of cigarettes or tobacco, but was also available for the taking on tables of fine restaurants, counters of cheap coffee shops, and in ashtrays of hotels and motels.

National distribution of these hidden persuaders promoting various popular consumer products was possible because of the proven worth of advertising. Free matches were an immediate success, and many companies began to allocate funds for displaying their products on matchbook covers. It was also Traute who approached William Wrigley with the idea of using matchcovers for advertising his company's product—chewing gum. Wrigley complied with an order for a billion matchbooks! The designs of Wrigley's art director and illustrator Otis G. Shepherd graced most of those matchbooks and remain collectible examples within the hobby.

Between 1920 and 1945, literally hundreds of billions of matchbooks were produced at a fraction of a cent per unit.

They varied in size, number of "strikes," design, and quality. At the peak of production, more than one hundred match companies were competing with one another for the business of advertisers. Vigorous competition spurred on greater efforts toward artistry and originality, bringing about marked results in a short time for advertisers as well as luring collectors into action. The largest companies to produce collectible covers were Diamond, Lion, Atlas, Universal, D.D. Bean, Ohio Match Company, Match Corporation of America, Federal, Superior, and Monarch.

Book matches were made from a cardboard or paperboard base that was cut into strips, called combs, of approximately one hundred

matches each. The heads of the matchsticks were dipped into a solution comprised of as many as twenty-five different chemicals for easy strikability, much the same as Joshua Pusey's early match was made. The cover designs were printed, using a rubber-plate process, onto sheets of cardboard that were wide enough to be cut into half-a-dozen matchbook covers. Each match company could supply designs for these covers from their own in-house art department, and artists could either pick up existing stock cuts or design artwork from scratch. Many illustrations were custom-made for clients based upon some photo reference, such as a hotel facade, for instance, or a company logo supplied by the client. The

process of simplification in reducing an advertisement or piece of artwork down to such small sizes, while maintaining the full range of color and attraction was the subtle beauty of the matchcover. Although commercial, this art-form was pure in that it espoused the innocence of its time. The matchcover was the naive art of American popular culture.

During World War II many match companies went out of business or merged with others due to stiff competition and dwindling supplies of raw materials. Even individuals tried matchbook advertising after World War II, when, due to the increased demand for housing by our returning military, many families could not find apartments. They told about their needs on matchbook covers and got results.

Today, with the wide use of reusable and disposable lighters, fewer than twenty companies produce all the matches used in the United States. Before warnings by the American Surgeon General were added to cigarette packs and advertising over the last two decades, smoking was considered a pleasurable pastime. Since this happened there has been a significant decline

in the number of Americans smoking, but the matchbook as an advertising medium for restaurants, bars, and boutiques has never been more popular.

This mini-artform survives, but not in the numbers and colors that were once produced. In spite of printing quality limitations, vintage matchbooks still stand as "striking" examples of early graphics in both simplicity and design.

COLLECTING MATCHCOVERS

There is a bit of the collector in all of us. No matter how big the collectible or how small, how many in the collection or how few, how important or how incidental the quest, almost everyone collects something. Collectors of the mini-artform of matchbook covers are known as "phillumenists," or "lovers of light," and, according to them, theirs is the second-largest hobby in the world—behind stamps. This claim is surely true if one can include those who automatically accumulated matchbooks from stores, restaurants, bars, and motels over the years. While their collections are usually found in drawers, boxes, or brandy snifters around the house, the true phillumenist carefully organizes

his assorted matchbooks and first "shucks" them. To "shuck" a matchbook, one removes the matches from the outer cover after carefully prying open the binding staple. Then the covers are categorized and cataloged according to subject matter, size, era, maker, or specialty and pressed into albums. Phillumenists do not collect matchbooks. They collect matchcovers. The only exceptions are those who collect the novelty matchcovers known as "features." This category constitutes designs that were featured on the flat matchsticks themselves, either as a repeated design on individual sticks or as a scene spread across the face of all the matches. These must be safeguarded more than any other category because of the very real possibility of seeing a collection go up in smoke.

Organized matchcover collecting took shape in the late 1920s, but it played second fiddle to the efforts of label savers in that era. In 1936 the Blue Moon Club, a label outfit, was rocked to its foundations when its president, W.W. Wilson, urged admission of matchcover addicts. Wilson seceded and set up his own group, which is rated as the forerunner of present collectors' organizations. Only two were

nationals—the United Matchonians, founded in 1936, and the Rathkamp Matchcover Society, founded on September 12, 1941. Inspired by the availability of free matchbooks at the 1939 New York World's Fair exhibits, Henry Rathkamp and a group of enthusiasts proposed an annual convention for matchcover collectors. The event was held later that year at Henry's home in Newport, Rhode Island, where fifty matchcover collectors were his enthusiastic guests. Rathkamp died in 1940, but his friends perpetuated his idea and founded the Rathkamp Memorial

Society for Matchcover Collectors.

The hobby itself was well established by the early 1920s, but the idea of organizing collectors was not firmly rooted. None of the early clubs that pre-dated the Rathkamp Society still exist, but they each served as an important link in keeping interest and activity alive. Today, the Rathkamp Matchcover Society is the only national club in existence, and it boasts international members as well. This hobby provides correspondence, friendships, and a mutual diversion among people throughout the world.

There are no hard and fast rules for beginning, keeping, or maintaining a collection of matchcovers. You can begin with a phone number of an old flame scribbled on the inside of a matchcover, with a souvenir of a place once visited that holds fond memories, or simply with the utilitarian purpose of igniting cigarette or pipe tobacco. Whatever the source, the few become the many. What to do with the growing accumulation prompts the collector to limit himself to specific categories or areas of interest within the vast possibilities. The individuality and character of the collector shines through in his ability to personalize the matchcovers he collects. Giving a collection personal taste and style in turn adds value and wins awards within the clubs. The most valuable cover is that which is the most difficult to acquire and the rarest of its kind. A matchcover commemorating Charles Lindbergh's 1927 transatlantic flight takes that prize. Only two are known to exist, and one is in the private collection of Evelyn Hovious of San Francisco, California. Evelyn has collected matchcovers since World War I, and, though many have been given away or traded over the years, she has amassed over 5 million covers. Her comprehensive collection is one of the most valuable in the world.

Condition also adds tremendously to the value of a matchcover—that is, striker intact, flat, unused (with no staple most preferred), otherwise unmarred, carefully shucked and stored for easy classification and display, but never pasted into albums. It is also the old law of supply and demand that determines worth, but monetary figures are hard to place upon matchcovers. Most covers are simply traded among collectors; what one enthusiast may value another may find trash. Occasionally some covers are auctioned off at club meetings or conventions, but usually to raise money for the club or some other worthy cause. Sharing one's hobby with others of like interest is what collecting is all about; there is no reason to let one's collection gather dust in some forgotten closet. Please share with us the golden age of matchcover art—a matchless diversion.

One of the greatest selling tools of the advertising trade was the matchbook. From the mid-1920s through the late '50s, millions of businesses made the public aware of their products through the use of this compact ad format. Full-color images enhanced the salability of everything from soft drinks to chewing gum, from roofing to haberdashery. Since the matches were not usually thrown away until all of the sticks were used, the graphics employed on the printable surfaces were subliminal reinforcements used up to twenty times, making matchcovers the first of the hidden persuaders.

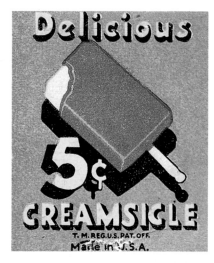

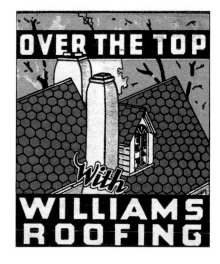

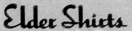

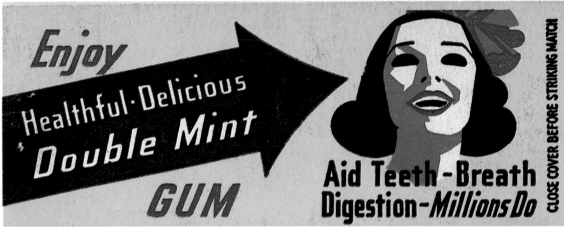

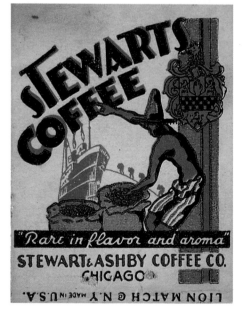

CHAMPIONS USE CHAMPIONS

Made in U.S.A.
THE DIAMOND MATCH CO. N.Y.C.

Don't Gamble!
5¢ DRINK 5¢
NATURAL SET UP
COPYRIGHT 1937 BY NATURAL SET UP SALES CORPORATION

BACK Guarantee
SYNOSCOPE
WORKS WONDERS
FOR HEAD
AILMENTS
SYN-O-SCOPE
LAB. INC.
CHICAGO
CLOSE COVER BEFORE STRIKING MATCH

FLAMING
YOUTH
FOR EVERY CAR

CHAMPION
SPARK PLUGS

Made in U.S.A.
THE DIAMOND MATCH CO. N.Y.C.

Soothe throat
VICKS
MEDICATED
Cough Drops

1935
MACHINE

CLEVELAND
SEPT. 11-21
TOOL
SHOW

RCA VICTOR
MAGIC BRAIN · MAGIC
EYE · METAL TUBES

The wild and woolly West was an advertiser's dream. The colorful landscape and masculine image of stern-faced Indian chiefs and heroic buckaroos served as mythic reminders of an American past often existing mostly in art departments' collective memory. Most prevalent as a theme in the Western part of the United States, where images of Conestogas and coy cowgirls made the most sense, the notion of the old frontier was so ingrained in the American fabric through motion pictures and pulp magazines that even chewing gum from Ohio and restaurants in Manhattan comfortably employed that look to sell their product. For them, the West was truly the best.

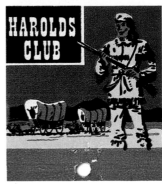

Visit
GLACIER
NATIONAL
PARK
JUNE 15
to
SEPT. 15

Made A.
THE DIAMOND CH CO. N.Y.C.

HOTEL BANNOCK

POCATELLO IDAHO
S.E.BRADY MANAGER

Soboba
Mineral
HOT
SPRINGS

San Jacinto
CALIFORNIA

Design & Mechanical Patents Pending
BIG Chief WAHOO

CHEWING GUM
4 STICKS for 1¢

CHICLE Ad. Corp., TOLEDO, O.

see RENO
HAROLDS
CLUB

CLOSE COVER BEFORE STRIKING

APACHE BAR
AND
COCKTAIL-
LOUNGE

LAS VEGAS, NEVADA

23

Shorts *and* Sweet!

*W*herever the male gender was to turn up, alluring damsels were available on countertops, free for the taking with immediate use in mind or for later admiration. Businesses could always rely on pin-ups by George Petty or Alberto Vargas to effectively sell their products, whether they were tires or tools, floor shows or fashions. Wartime maidens straddled bombs and bare-breasted gals posed seductively, hinting at forbidden pleasures that a matchcover owner might discover if only he heeded the advertiser's message to come see or use his product. Plain and simple, the timeless message being offered was that SEX sells.

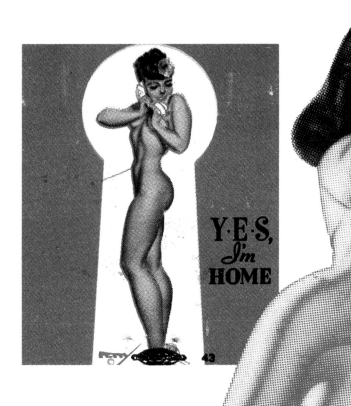

Y·E·S, I'm HOME

PISTOL PACKIN MAMMA!

MONARCH MATCH CO.,"SAN JOSE,"CALIF.

Here's LOOKING at you!!

Snug as a Bug

ANY NUMBER— I'M LONESOME!

A HAIR RAISING LINE

Strictly for MEN

(SEE INSIDE)

CLOSE COVER BEFORE STRIKING

PARA-CUTIE

Rube Kolker's All Girl Revue

BLUE ROOM

CLOSE · COVER · BEFORE · STRIKING

Turn night into PLAY at Mitchell's ☆ LET'S HAVE A DRINK AND SEE WHAT HAPPENS

400 N. WABASH AVE. CHICAGO

RIO CABANA

CLOSE COVER BEFORE STRIKING

HERCULES DON'T MISS

CLOSE · COVER · BEFORE · STRIKING

COCKTAILS · ENTERTAINMENT

Chop Suey Chow Mein Fried Shrimp

CLOSE COVER BEFORE STRIKING

Jantzen
FAMOUS FOR
SUN CLOTHES
FOUNDATIONS

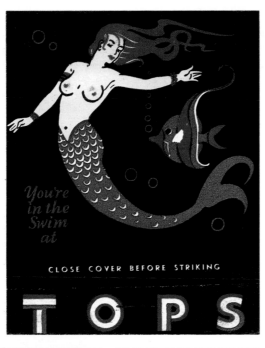

You're in the Swim at

CLOSE COVER BEFORE STRIKING

TOPS

Close Cover Before Striking

STARTLING TROPICAL STORMS

shows every hour

TROPICS SHOWS ARE A
STAND OUT IN AMERICA

CLUB
U-GENE

THE TROPICS
ATMOSPHERE
DOES
SOMETHING
for EVERYBODY

CLOSE COVER BEFORE STRIKING

32

Trains were said to run faster than speeding bullets. Graceful ocean liners plied vast seas. The open road beckoned travelers by bus and car. Whatever the mode, transportation was a preoccupation of Americans during the first half of the twentieth century, and matchcovers were natural for purveying America's new wonders of the mechanical age. Not only could they sell the practical, such as used cars or coal, but, incorporating images such as streamlined clipper ships of the air, they could be used to suggest faraway destinations—even if the establishment in question was the corner bar or local diner. The matchbook was brought home more often as a keepsake of a location visited than for everyday use.

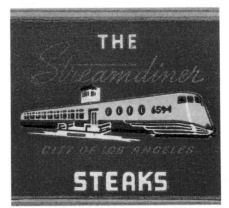

UNITED STATES SHIP WEST VIRGINIA

NORMANDIE
THE WORLD'S LARGEST SHIP

KNUTSEN LINE

CLOSE COVER BEFORE STRIKING

UNITED STATES LINES

DECKS *mean* COMFORT, SAFETY, CONVENIENCE

JOHANNA SMITH II

McCORMICK

THE 7 SEAS

35

"TAKE OFF"

FROM THE
CHANCELLOR
Clipper Ship
CLOSE COVER BEFORE STRIKING

Only Experts Mix Our Drinks

DINING
AND
DANCING

FREE INSIDE PARKING
NEVER A COUVERT

PANAMA
INK CONTROL

MANUFACTURED BY
MANIFOLD SUPPLIES CO.
BROOKLYN, N.Y.
CLOSE COVER BEFORE STRIKING

WORLD FAMOUS
Kitty Davis
AIRLINER
MIAMI BEACH, FLORIDA
CLOSE COVER BEFORE STRIKING

LA GUARDIA FIELD RESTAURANTS

NEW YORK MUNICIPAL AIRPORT

THE CHINA CLIPPER

COCKTAILS

MID-CONTINENT
Airlines

uses
TEXACO
GASOLINE, OIL, GREASE
exclusively
FEDERAL MATCH CORP. NEW YORK

CLOSE COVER BEFORE STRIKING

Who could resist a night's lodging in a grand edifice bathed in klieg lights or perched handsomely above a seaside cliff? Hotel owners took no chances with the visuals they splashed on the matchcovers so generously given away. A variety of comforts and services could easily be extolled, hopefully reaching future visitors as well as reminding current guests to return for the pleasures they enjoyed while staying there. The covers also served as rate cards and in some cases revealed the locations of other hospices in a motel chain. All in all, the message of the match to the kings and queens of the road was "Have a nice night."

LA FONDA-IN OLD SANTA FÉ, NEW MEXICO

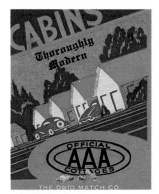

CABINS
Thoroughly Modern

OFFICIAL AAA COTTAGES

THE OHIO MATCH CO.

NEAREST HIGH SIERRA RESORT TO SOUTHERN CALIFORNIA

GLACIER LODGE
BIG PINE, Inyo Co., CALIFORNIA
Elevation 8,000 Ft.

CLOSE · COVER · BEFORE · STRIKING

FRANK TORRES
MARINE VIEW HOTEL

MOSS BEACH, CALIF.

CLOSE COVER BEFORE STRIKING

GRANDE COURTS

AMERICA'S FINEST
TOURIST QUARTERS

BILTMORE MOTOR INN

11827 VENTURA BLVD.
NORTH HOLLYWOOD, CALIF.- U.S. ROUTE #101 NORTH

For the business with a limited budget and a broad-based commodity to sell, stock cuts were available to advertisers through a match-cover salesman's catalog. From simple designs to more elaborate ones, everything under the sun could be sold using existing drawings, saving the time and money normally spent on a custom job. Public service messages were always popular, confirming an advertiser's commitment to his customer and thus avoiding the hard sell. Whatever the product, stock cuts could provide the appropriate graphic in full color or black and white to make any establishment worthy of a million-dollar clientele.

EVERYTHING IN HOME APPLIANCES

P.A.P.
LOYAL ORDER OF MOOSE

A FRATERNAL ORGANIZATION OF THE HIGHEST INTEGRITY

IMPORTED & DOMESTIC

WINES & LIQUORS

FUNERAL DIRECTOR

REASONABLE · DEPENDABLE

SeaFood

OUR SPECIALTY

CHOICE WINES and LIQUORS

Groceries STAPLE and FANCY

BREAD

Matchcover art soared to grand heights with its application to eating establishments. Layer upon layer of color gave owners a chance to display their immaculate buildings and taste-tempting cuisine. Waiters sang, chefs offered platters of food, and service was supreme. On some covers palm trees swayed while on others lurid Oriental scenes beckoned diners into exotic settings they would never experience at their own dining room tables. These mini-billboards promised more than just a dining sensation; it was a trip around the world, a chance to hobnob with the "swells," or dance the hula on a tropical isle. All of this was tucked away in a pocket-sized convenience, free for the asking.

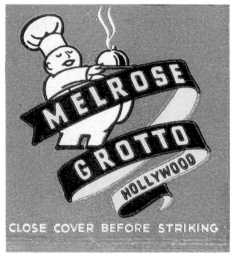

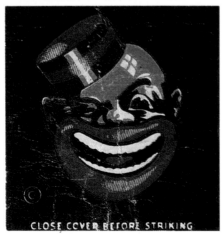

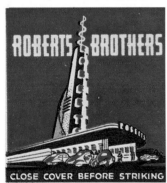

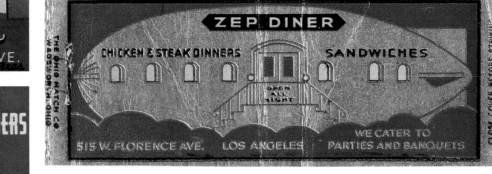

THE HURRICANE

IN THE INTERNATIONAL SETTLEMENT
533 PACIFIC AVE.
SAN FRANCISCO

CLOSE COVER BEFORE STRIKING

PAGE

131 EAST FIRST ST.
LONG BEACH.
CALIF.

CLOSE COVER BEFORE STRIKING MATCH

Tropical
CAFETERIA

MALIBAR

10663 W. PICO BLVD.
WEST LOS ANGELES

THE
CHI-CHI
BAR & GRILL

Avalon, Santa Catalina

PETER'S Grill

85 SOUTH NINTH STREET

MINNEAPOLIS

CLOSE COVER BEFORE STRIKING

RICKETT'S

103 E. CHICAGO AVE.

CLOSE COVER BEFORE STRIKING

McDONNELL'S

FINE FOOD and COCKTAILS

MERLE'S DRIVE IN

BARBECUED MEATS
FOUNTAIN SERVICE

2602 AMERICAN AVE.
LONG BEACH, CALIFORNIA
PHONE 912-43

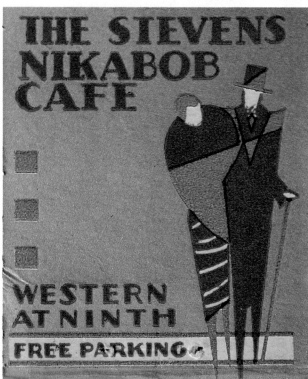

THE STEVENS NIKABOB CAFE

WESTERN AT NINTH

FREE PARKING

Nickodell

Nickodell

"FIT FOR A KING"
PRINCE'S famous HAMBURGERS

HOUSTON
BEAUMONT
DALLAS
SAN ANTONIO

DINE DANCE ROMANCE

The HOUSE OF SINGING WAITERS

PARIS INN

210 EAST MARKET ST.
LOS ANGELES

GINGERS CAFE

2913 UNIVERSITY
SAN DIEGO

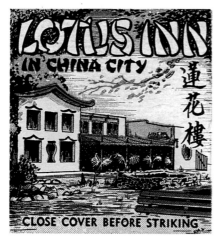

For an additional cost advertisers could go whole hog and order the next step in matchcover art. Prized by collectors for their unique configurations and novel appearances, "features" were in a class by themselves. Any subject could be incorporated onto the matchstick itself. Soldiers, cigarettes, bombs, and frolicking nudes were lined up inside the matchcover, representing an amazing array of products. Innovative uses for the striking area, known in the trade as "spot-strikers," resulted in strange and wonderful surfaces for match-striking. Even special die-cuts added interest and caught the eye. It was no wonder so many of these beauties ended up unused, preserved for future admiration.

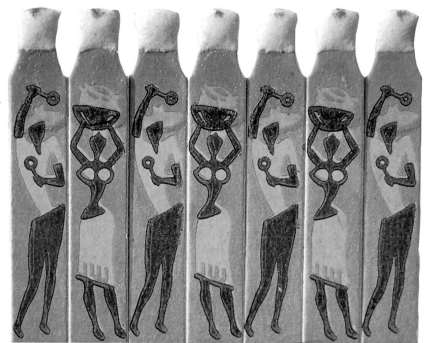

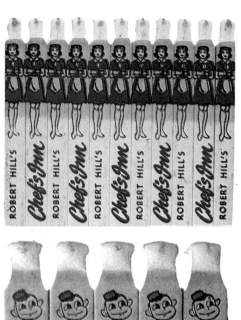

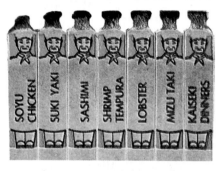

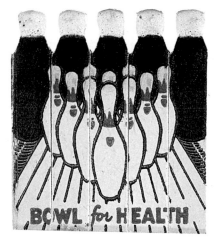

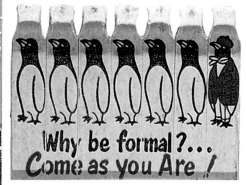

BOWL 16 LANES

Emil's

BARBER SHOP

Reservations SP 4-9808

LUNCHES   DINNERS

COCKTAILS

MAN'S SIZE SANDWICHES

DOWNTOWN BOWL

ORdway
3-6977

EDDY at JONES
SAN FRANCISCO

MORALE needs AMUSEMENT

Village Smoke Shop

A nation at war, a campaign to win, or a simple confirmation of just how great it is to be an American—whatever the cause, patriotic matchcovers rose to the occasion. Politicians found the inexpensive advertising perfectly suited to their election needs. Every time a match was struck a candidate would stick in the voter's mind, hopefully until he reached the polling booth. In the wartime era of the 1940s, civilians were reminded to save scrap, buy bonds, and keep their lips sealed. Jumping on the bandwagon, advertisers saw to it that their messages echoed these sentiments and confirmed that they were patriots, too. It was an America united; it was a democracy at work, and there were matches to be lit.

FRANKLIN D. ROOSEVELT
CLOSE COVER BEFORE STRIKING MATCH

FOR PEACE AND PROSPERITY

Stick WITH IKE

CLOSE COVER BEFORE STRIKING

WOODROW WILSON
CLOSE COVER BEFORE STRIKING MATCH

FOR PRESIDENT

The RESIDENCE of PRESIDENTS
CLOSE COVER BEFORE STRIKING MATCH

VOTE FOR

HERBERT HOOVER   CHARLES CURTIS

ELECT AL SMITH

U. S. ARMY AIR BASE

HAMMER FIELD

FRESNO, CALIF.

CLOSE COVER BEFORE STRIKING

Okla. 3 WILL ROGERS FIELD

CLOSE COVER BEFORE STRIKING

Through the movies the whole world knew the faces of their stars and those legendary places where they worked and played, in Tinseltown and along the Great White Way: the Stork Club, the Hollywood Bowl, and the Copacabana. As on miniature tabloids, the celluloid images of the stars were plastered on matchbooks, and studios issued paeans to their own self-importance in the industry. The latest movie was presented on thousands of matchcovers and distributed to an adoring public. Glamor spots and night clubs inspired visions of dreamy moonlit nights, sophisticated chatter, romantic dancing, and, of course, Hollywood—the land of everybody's dreams.

Katharine Hepburn

CLOSE COVER BEFORE STRIKING MATCH

Fred Astaire

CLOSE COVER BEFORE STRIKING MATCH

Jean Harlow

CLOSE COVER BEFORE STRIKING MATCH

Clark Gable

CLOSE COVER BEFORE STRIKING MATCH

80

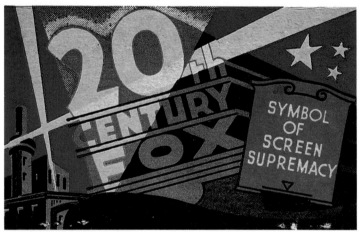

20th CENTURY FOX

SYMBOL OF SCREEN SUPREMACY

Universal International Pictures

Jack Oakie

CLOSE COVER BEFORE STRIKING MATCH

Harriet Hilliard

CLOSE COVER BEFORE STRIKING MATCH

Douglas Fairbanks, Jr.

CLOSE COVER BEFORE STRIKING MATCH

Jean Arthur

CLOSE COVER BEFORE STRIKING MATCH

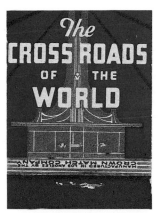

The irresistible icon of a tuxedoed pig and his equally debonair poultry date were prime reasons for incorporating the animal kingdom into matchcover imagery. The charm of winking simians, dancing clams, and high-kicking mules was a sure-fire, eye-catching device used to lure customers. Along with the more whimsical identities came the assorted familiar logos that utilized a Noah's ark of characters, made more dynamic by a variety of bold colors and patterns emblazoned on the printed surface. The endearing concept of animals as pets brought life and a sense of humor to products and businesses alike.

84

Comfortably COOL

"His Master's Choice"

CALO DOG FOOD FOR ALL DOGS

ORIOLE CAFETERIAS

HERCULES GASOLINE

has the KICK

THE RECORD BREAKER

GILMORE

RED LION GASOLINE

NOT CARBONATED

REAL FRUIT BEVERAGES

SEA FOOD GROTTO

DETROIT'S EXCLUSIVE SEA FOOD RESTAURANT
212 W. GRAND RIVER AVE. HOTEL GRISWOLD BLDG.

HAMILTON STORES INC.
CLOSE COVER BEFORE STRIKING MATCH

POLLY GAS

SKILLED VETERINARIAN

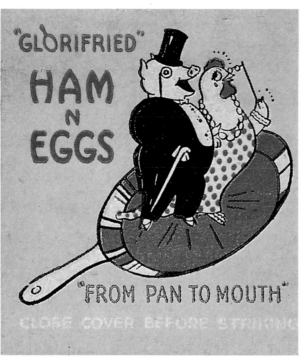

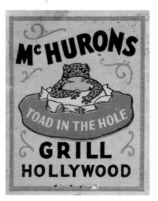

From the turn of the century until the mid-1950s, numerous international expositions were rich sources for collectible matchcover products. Not only did the expositions themselves issue covers, but the sponsoring industries, countries, and pavilions created bold graphics that were some of the era's best. The application of these designs to matchcovers signaled a high-water mark in the art of the matchcover in both graphics and printing. Visitors from around the world gathered at these global events, pocketing souvenirs to be used and remembered.

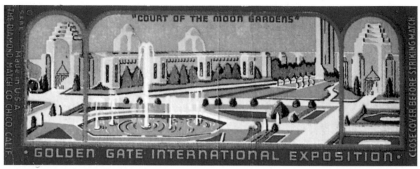

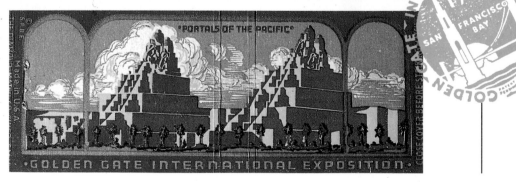

Come and Enjoy· · · · · · a Delicious Treat

WRIGLEY'S SPEARMINT CHEWING GUM

The Flavor Lasts

HALL OF SCIENCE NORTH FACADE

COPYRIGHT 1932 BY "A CENTURY OF PROGRESS"

A CENTURY OF PROGRESS INTERNATIONAL EXPOSITION·CHICAGO·1933

THE HALL OF SCIENCE·TOWER

COPYRIGHT 1932 BY "A CENTURY OF PROGRESS"

A CENTURY OF PROGRESS INTERNATIONAL EXPOSITION CHICAGO·1933

NEW YORK 1939 WORLD'S FAIR

THE SOUTH TOWERS

90

The wide world of matchcovers for sports-men ranged from celebrity endorsements to the excitement of seeing a bowling damsel fallen on her derriere! Sports stars invested their lucrative salaries in real estate ventures such as restaurants, motels, and sports centers, and, to cash in on their fame and to increase business, their like-nesses were printed on that advertising workhorse—the matchcover. In between were placid scenes of pastel golf courses, athletically built skiers schussing down pristine slopes, or well-dressed trout fishermen netting the big one. Health addicts were encouraged to bowl. But even if you did noth-ing, perhaps you could still light up a stogie and dream about flexing the flesh.

HUNTINGTON PARK BOWLING CENTER

Fine Foods

2801-5 EAST SLAUSON AVE.-HUNTINGTON PARK, CALIF.

YOSEMITE PARK AND CURRY COMPANY

YOSEMITE WINTER SPORTS

JACK DEMPSEY KNOCKS OUT JESS WILLARD TOLEDO, O. JULY 4, 1919 AND BECOMES CHAMPION OF THE WORLD

GOLDEN ARM RESTAURANT

CLOSE COVER BEFORE STRIKING MATCH

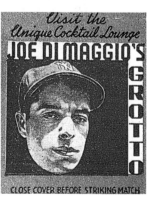

Visit the Unique Cocktail Lounge JOE DI MAGGIO'S GROTTO

CLOSE COVER BEFORE STRIKING MATCH

WonderBowl

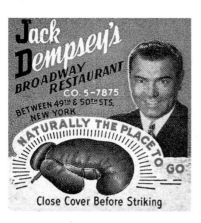

"BUCKETS" GOLDENBERG - PROP.

MATCHBOOK–The printed cardboard with matches attached by staple

MATCHCOVER–The outside printed cardboard without the matches

STEMS–Matchsticks or chemically coated pieces of cardboard

STRIKER–An abrasive strip affixed to front of matchcover

REVERSE STRIKER–An abrasive strip affixed to back of match-cover; a.k.a. an S.O.B.

SPOT STRIKER–A striker worked into the design of the matchcover

FEATURES–Wide, flat images printed directly on the matchsticks

CONTOUR–Die-cut matchcover in the shape of advertiser's product

FULL LENGTH–Matchcover design running entire length of front and back covers

SADDLE–Top section of match-book, joining front and back covers

SHUCK–Removal of matches from cover by carefully prying open staple

BOBTAIL–A matchcover without any striker, from misuse or ignorance

MAKER MARK–Logo or mark of manufacturer on matchbook

GIRLIES–Pin-up girl matchcovers, by well-known calendar artists

USED BOOK–Matchbook that has a bitten, struck, or hit striker

PRESS–To flatten a matchcover before insertion into album

CADDY–A full box of 50 matchbooks; 50 caddies equal one case

FLATS–Unfolded printed matchcovers without staples; a.k.a. virgins

HUMMINGBIRD–Matchbook containing 8 lights

TEN-STRIKE–Matchbooklet containing 10 lights

MIDGET–Matchbook containing 14 lights

REGULAR–Matchbook containing the normal 20 lights

30-SIZE–Matchbook containing 30 matches

ROYAL FLASH–Matchbook twice the width of regular, containing 40 lights

FISHERMAN'S SPECIAL–Foot-long matchbook holding 300 matches

C.C.B.S.–Close cover before striking

94

Special thanks for the collections and research of Ruth and Thomas Hagan, Norman Moore, Gary Johns, Deborah Ross, Bill Thomas, Jeff Spielberg, Mitzi Bradbury, Danny Holloway, Louis and Marie Williams, Nancy Kintisch, Freda Wheatley-Vizcarra, Allene and Dennis Rose, Mike Koelker, Boe Nania, Steve Sakai, Brad Benedict, Walton Rawls, Stat House, and Andresen Typographics.

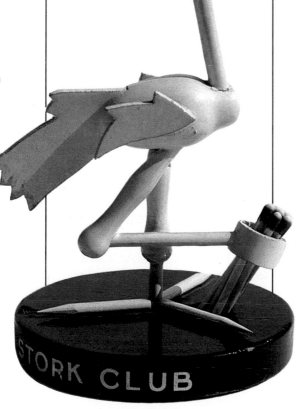

For further information on collecting and clubs:

Rathkamp Matchcover Society
c/o Emily Hiller
2501 W. Sunflower—#H5
Santa Ana, California 92704

Long Beach Matchcover Club
c/o Ruth Hagan
1330 10th Street
Santa Monica, California 90401

Windy City Matchcover Club
c/o Bob Cigrang
622 North Russell
Mt. Prospect, Illinois 60056

The Front Striker
c/o Bill Retskin
3417 Clayborne Ave.
Alexandria, Virginia 22306

THE END